The Medical Marvel

A Doctor's Guide to Thriving in the New Era

The Medical Marvel

A Doctor's Guide to Thriving in the New Era

Ramesh Chandra

Available on amazonkindle

Worldwide Published by

Pendown Press
PREMIUM BUSINESS PUBLISHER

PENDOWN PRESS LLP
An ISO 9001 & ISO 14001 Certified Co.,
Regd. Office: 3767A, Kanhaiya Nagar,
Tri Nagar, Delhi-110035
Ph.: 8130886000, 9650072927
E-mail: info@pendownpress.com
Branch Office: 1A/2A, 20, Hari Sadan, Ansari Road,
Daryaganj, New Delhi-110002
Ph.: 011-45794768
Website: PendownPress.com

Edition: 2025
Price: ₹ 399
ISBN: 978-93-7217-860-9

Layout Designed by Pendown Graphics Team
Cover Designed by Naina Baindur
Printed and Bound in India by Thomson Press India Ltd.

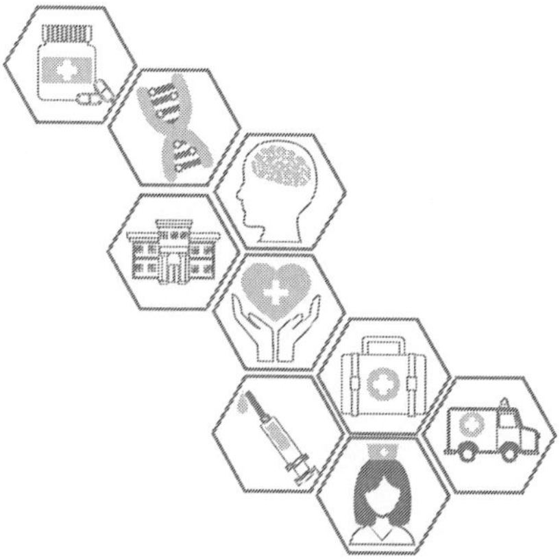

The Medical Marvel

A Practical Guide to Thriving in Modern Healthcare

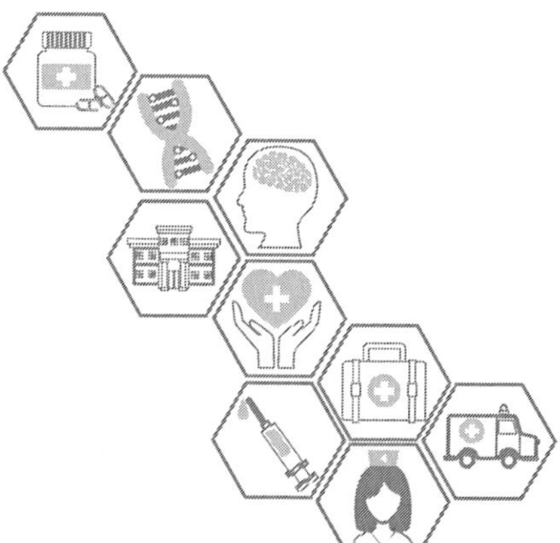

Disclaimer

The information contained in *The Medical Marvel: A Practical Guide to Thriving in Modern Healthcare* is provided for general educational and informational purposes only. It is not intended as, and should not be relied upon as, a substitute for professional medical, legal, financial, or regulatory advice. Readers are strongly encouraged to consult qualified professionals regarding any specific circumstances, medical concerns, business decisions, or compliance requirements.

The author has made every effort to ensure the accuracy and reliability of the information presented. However, healthcare regulations, technologies, and best practices evolve continuously, and the author makes no representations or warranties regarding the completeness, timeliness, or applicability of the content. Neither the author nor the publisher shall be held liable for any direct, indirect, incidental, or consequential damages, losses, or risks that may arise from the use or misuse of the information contained in this book.

Any case studies, examples, or anecdotes provided are illustrative in nature. References to individuals, organizations, or platforms do not imply endorsement. Patient-related examples have been anonymized or are used with permission, and no confidential information has been disclosed.

By reading this book, the reader acknowledges that they are responsible for their own decisions and actions in applying any of the strategies, tools, or recommendations described herein.

TABLE OF CONTENTS

Acknowledgements		i
Preface		iii
Chapter 1	: The Crisis No One Talks About	**1**
Chapter 2	: The Power of Personal Branding for Doctors	**7**
Chapter 3	: Building a Thriving Practice: Systems, Not Stress	**15**
Chapter 4	: Lifelong Learning: Staying Relevant in Medicine	**25**
Chapter 5	: Ethical Digital Presence: Earning Trust Online	**31**
Chapter 6	: Setting Up Operations That Scale: Your Third Step	**39**
Chapter 7	: Patient Engagement: Connecting Beyond Care	**45**
Chapter 8	: Platforms to Connect: Online & Offline Strategies	**51**
Chapter 9	: The Business of Healing: Finances & Growth	**59**
Chapter 10	: Sustaining the Healer: Well-being, Balance, and Looking Ahead	**63**
Blueprint to Growth		71

Bhawar Lal Choudhary

A true Source of Inspiration and Wisdom, the guiding force behind my courage, clarity and purpose.

ACKNOWLEDGEMENTS

My heart's deepest gratitude goes to my parents, who have been the true pillars of my life. Both are incredible people who not only worked tirelessly to give us a good education but also showed us unconditional love by easily forgiving even our biggest mistakes. Their comforting words: "Don't worry beta, time will change, work again", have been my guiding light, reminding me that no challenge is permanent when faith and effort walk together.

My heart is overflowing with gratitude for my family, whose love has been my anchor throughout this journey. My wife, Sangeeta Choudhary, and our children have given me unwavering love and support. They have stood by me through every late night, every difficult decision, and every triumph. Their belief in me and the warm home we share kept me grounded and motivated, even when the path was unclear.

I owe a debt of gratitude to my brother, Dinesh Kumar, his wife H. Santhosh, and their children. During my darkest times, when I felt lost and unsure of what to do next, it was their encouragement and faith that lifted me up. They reminded me of my worth and pushed me to take action when hope seemed out of reach. Because of them, I learned that no challenge is insurmountable when you have family by your side.

My business partner and inspiration, Bhawar Lal Choudhary, truly deserves special recognition. I fondly think of Bhawar Lal Choudhary as "the person who is above the sky," for his sky-high optimism and generosity. He believed in my vision even when I doubted myself and constantly inspired me to move forward and reach higher. His trust in me has been a powerful gift, pushing our partnership to new heights and teaching me to always dream bigger.

I am deeply thankful to my coaches, Rajiv Talreja and Karan Hasija, for the invaluable lessons they have shared with me. They have taught me the importance of building strong business systems, creating effective teams, and setting clear processes. From them, I have learned how to run a business independently and confidently. Their guidance has been a guiding light in building the foundation of my work.

A special thanks goes to Sidra Jafri, who introduced me to the simple yet profound truth that "Everything is energy." This insight transformed my outlook on life and work, helping me to see challenges and opportunities in a new light. I am grateful for her wisdom and the fresh perspective she gave me during a time of growth.

I could never have written this book or made the progress I have without each of you. Through some of the most difficult and transformative phases of my life, your love, faith, and guidance have carried me forward. This book is as much yours as it is mine, and I am forever grateful to have you all by my side. Thank you for believing in me.

PREFACE

Throughout my journey across India, I have had the privilege of working with thousands of doctors, remarkable professionals who pour their hearts into treating their patients. Their dedication is undeniable, and their knowledge and expertise are unmatched. Yet, there is a challenge I have observed time and time again: despite their commitment to patient care, many doctors struggle with managing and growing their clinics or hospitals effectively.

As I've worked with these incredible individuals, I've learned that running a clinic or hospital is far more than just treating patients—it's about managing the intricate operations that make it run smoothly, making strategic decisions that set the practice up for long-term success, and building a brand that leaves a lasting impact. The truth is, most doctors are so focused on their patients that they overlook these crucial aspects. They work tirelessly day in and day out, but fail to think about the bigger picture—how to elevate their practices to a national or even international level.

Too often, I've heard doctors say, "Without my presence, my clinic or hospital cannot run." And while their passion is admirable, this belief becomes a limiting factor in their growth. I've asked them, "But what about established healthcare brands like Manipal, CIMS, or Columbia Asia? How do they scale and thrive without being solely dependent on one person?" The answer is always the same: silence.

Unfortunately, many doctors fail to consider the possibility of building a sustainable brand that isn't reliant on their personal presence.

The reality is, effective marketing, strategic branding, and management systems can take a practice to unimaginable heights. Yet, many doctors still rely on outdated marketing methods—free health camps, pamphlets, and word-of-mouth—which, while valuable in the early stages, do not lead to sustainable growth. As a result, doctors often feel discouraged, believing their practice isn't good enough, and they settle into a cycle of stagnation.

Even when some doctors achieve success and attract a steady stream of patients, they often fail to take their practice to the next level. Some open multispecialty hospitals, but the brand is still tied to the doctor's personal name. The hospital becomes reliant on the doctor's presence, and without that presence, patients stop coming. This lack of a strong hospital brand prevents long-term growth and scalability.

Very few doctors in India have managed to create large, impactful healthcare brands that resonate on a national or international scale. Dr. Devi Shetty's Narayana Health is one of the rare examples of a brand that has expanded its reach, providing accessible, affordable, and quality care. But such examples remain few, and many doctors still struggle to build sustainable practices that outlive their personal presence.

This book is for those doctors who are ready to break free from the cycle of dependence on their personal brand. It is for those who want to build a practice that grows and thrives without their constant presence. I've had the privilege of learning from some of the best in marketing and branding, including Rajiv Talreja and Karan Hasija, and I want to share the insights, strategies, and tools I've gained to help you create a healthcare brand that can stand the test of time.

Throughout this book, we will explore the importance of consistent engagement, the power of marketing, and the value of building a brand that speaks to people even when they don't currently need your services. You'll learn how to position yourself as an authority, how to engage with your community, and how to create a brand that resonates in the minds of your patients. It's not just about getting more patients—it's about building a legacy.

As you read through the pages, I hope you feel inspired to take action. The journey ahead is one of transformation, not just for your practice, but for the future of healthcare. With the right tools, strategies, and mindset, your dream of creating a lasting, impactful brand is not only possible, it's achievable.

Let's embark on this journey together and create a healthcare brand that will not only change your practice but also the way people experience healthcare in India.

Let's begin the transformation.

My goal is to help you build a legacy practice that thrives **on systems and compassion**, not just your personal sacrifice. If you're ready to elevate your practice without working harder, welcome aboard. Your journey to becoming a true **Medical Marvel** starts here.

CHAPTER 1

THE CRISIS NO ONE TALKS ABOUT

> ***"In today's medicine, healing begins not with a prescription, but with a conversation. The future of care belongs to those who treat patients not just as cases, but as people."***

As a modern doctor, success isn't just measured by clinical skills or patient volume. Today's patients see healthcare as a holistic *service experience*. They want convenience, empathy, and clear communication at every step. For example, scheduling an appointment, getting lab results via an app, or receiving a simple follow-up text all shape how patients feel about their care. Surveys consistently show that communication is paramount: over 70% of patients say they highly value doctors who explain things clearly. Conversely, a lack of empathy drives people away—research indicates 83% of patients would switch providers after a poor communication experience. In short, **patients are in the driver's seat**, and they vote with their feet (or clicks).

At the same time, doctors today wear **multiple hats**. You are a Healer, but also a Communicator, Organizer, Ethical Educator, and even a Tech-Savvy Leader. Each role contributes to the success of your practice:

- **Healer:** Your core role is to diagnose and treat patients using evidence-based medicine.
- **Communicator:** Bridge the gap between complex medical info and what your patients understand.
- **Organizer:** Streamline operations so that appointments, billing, and records run smoothly without chaos.
- **Ethical Educator:** Provide patient-first health education (avoid grandiose claims) and always respect consent and confidentiality.
- **Tech Leader:** Embrace simple technologies (smartphone apps, automated reminders, EMRs) that free your time and improve care.

Clarity and Empathy

Patient care today is as much about emotional intelligence as it is medical know-how. Patients want to *feel* heard and cared for. Something as simple as a warm greeting at reception or a handwritten note of encouragement can build loyalty. One study of millions of patient comments found that 85% of remarks about clinicians were positive when kindness was present, but 83% of patients would leave after a single dismissive experience. As one wise physician said, "Kindness is not a soft skill; in healthcare, it's a survival skill."

Practical Communication Strategies

You can start improving patient interactions today with small, deliberate steps:

- **Speak Human, Not Medical:** Replace jargon with plain language. For instance, say "a kind of bacteria in your stomach" instead of "H. pylori". Imagine explaining conditions to your own family.

- **Use Teach-Back:** After explaining a plan, ask the patient to repeat it back to you in their own words. ("Can you tell me how you'll take this medicine?") This verifies understanding and highlights any confusion immediately.
- **Visuals and Analogies:** Draw simple sketches or use models. A quick diagram of a knee or a printed anatomy chart can make complex ideas click. Even a short explainer video played in the clinic or shared on WhatsApp empowers patients.
- **Bite-Sized Info:** Limit each conversation to 3 key points. If a diabetic patient is visiting, focus on their blood sugar goal, one medication adjustment, and the next lab tests. Overloading information at once often means nothing is remembered.
- **Language Matters:** Whenever possible, speak in the patient's mother tongue or simplest English. Keep printed instructions ("Take on an empty stomach", "Next appointment date") in local languages.
- **Invite Questions:** Encourage an open dialogue. Say something like, "Please ask any questions; no question is too small." Make it safe to admit confusion.

Beyond the Clinic: Designing the Patient Journey

Think like a guest at a hotel or a shopper on Amazon – healthcare should feel easy, not Administrative. Map out your patient's entire experience, from first contact to follow-up:

- **Streamline Scheduling:** Offer online booking links (Google, your website, WhatsApp bot) or a clear phone protocol. Send automated reminders with all details (date, time, prep instructions) well in advance. Many clinics cut no-show rates dramatically by sending two-way SMS/ WhatsApp reminders.

- **Front-Desk Warmth:** Train receptionists to greet patients by name, explain any wait times, and use positive language. Digital pre-registration forms (Google Forms or simple clinic apps) can save time at check-in. Greeting the patient by name will impact your brand in the most positive way instead of a token number. People feel happy when they are called by their name, and most with the proper pronunciation. If you can't pronounce a word, you can ask a patient.
- **Smooth Waiting Area:** Display a Name system or a board with current patient numbers. If you don't have sufficient space to wait. Allow patients to wait outside or in a car – send an SMS when you're ready to see them. If visiting any clinic or hospital whose environment is not good and non-hygienic, would you prefer to go again?
- **Meaningful Follow-Ups:** Treat follow-up as genuine care. Schedule the next visit before patients leave and send a confirming reminder a few days prior. After each visit, have your system auto-send a summary of the diagnosis, prescriptions, and next steps via SMS or WhatsApp.
- **Digital Access:** Email or text copies of prescriptions and lab results. Encourage patients to save these in a file or health app. This reduces confusion and repeated calls.
- **24/7 Support:** Provide clear instructions for emergencies on your website or clinic board. Set up an on-call number or a WhatsApp FAQ auto-reply for after-hours questions. Even a short automated message ("We'll get back to you soon!") reassures patients.

Feedback as a Mirror

You can't improve what you don't measure. Collect patient feedback routinely (suggestion box, QR code surveys, WhatsApp polls).

Ask simple questions: "Did we explain things clearly?", "Was your wait time reasonable?", "How would you rate your visit?". Review this data monthly in team meetings. Celebrate compliments publicly (post reviews on a bulletin board and address complaints privately. By treating feedback as a gift, you'll continually refine your practice.

Key Takeaways

- Modern patients expect more than medical expertise – they want respect, clarity, and empathy at every turn.
- By improving communication (e.g., *speaking their language*, using teach-back), streamlining processes (better scheduling, reminders), and listening actively, you turn routine visits into healing experiences.
- These steps not only boost loyalty and outcomes but make your work far more rewarding.

Remember, you already have the hardest part down: clinical skill. Now apply that intelligence to **how you deliver care.** Small changes – a friendlier greeting, a quick follow-up text, a clear explanation – build a reputation that patients trust and cherish.

CHAPTER 2

THE POWER OF PERSONAL BRANDING FOR DOCTOR

"If a patient googled my name right now, would they find the doctor I want to be?"

This question hits home in our digital era. With over **80% of people using Google** before choosing a doctor, and more than **70% of Indian patients reporting that social media posts influence health** decisions, **visibility is credibility**. In practice, that means your expertise only matters if patients can find and trust you online.

Why Branding Matters

Branding isn't vanity; it's trust-building. Think of your online presence as a digital waiting room. A well-maintained website or Google Business profile is like a warm clinic lobby before a patient even arrives. It's not about advertising treatments; it's about putting caring, accurate information at their fingertips. Statistics confirm this shift: one survey found that **only 40% of adults trust physicians and hospitals** (down from 71% in 2020), highlighting a general erosion of trust. But Indian patients remain engaged: a study showed over

82% use platforms like WhatsApp, YouTube, and Facebook to learn about health. By sharing quality information yourself, you meet them where they are, reinforcing trust.

Core Principle – Caring Before Selling

Always start with service. India's medical councils emphasize ethical, patient-focused outreach (no false guarantees). A hospital COO put it well: genuine patient moments (like a nurse calmly explaining a child's procedure) build brand trust more than flashy ads. So when you post or speak, think "doctor advising a friend," not "company making a sale."

1. **Patient-First Content:** Create health education, not sales copy. Example: Dr. Sharma in Bangalore wrote simple blog posts on diabetes and saw far more engagement than he ever did with an advertisement. Answer real patient questions. If you notice many patients ask "How to manage diabetes?", write an FAQ-style post or record a short video (even 2–3 minutes) answering that question in plain language. Use analogies ("Your lungs are like two bellows") and avoid jargon. Share patient stories (with permission) to show real impact. Take Action: Survey patients briefly or simply listen to their questions to find top topics. Then write or record one helpful post per week addressing those needs.
2. **Be Genuine & Transparent:** Exaggerations are a trap. If you **promise a "100% cure,"** you'll only lose credibility. Instead, speak honestly. For example, a surgeon who openly explained both risks and benefits of a procedure found patients trusted him more, not less. In your content, clarify what a treatment can realistically do: **e.g., "This therapy helps 70% of patients feel better, though some may need additional care"**. Admit what you don't know. Consider a brief behind-the-scenes post: a day in your

clinic, or a photo of your team. Answer patient questions from your inbox or comment section openly – this builds rapport.

3. **Respect Privacy & Consent:** This is non-negotiable. Always anonymize patient stories and get written permission for any testimonials or photos.

   Treat data like gold – lock personal info away, use secure messaging for sharing test results, and never share identifiable details without consent. Patients will thank you for the respect, and it avoids ethical pitfalls. Take Action: Check one piece of patient-related content you've shared online. Do you have permission? If not, delete it and update your content checklist to always include a consent step.

4. **Engage, Don't Broadcast:** Social media and **online forums are communities, not billboards.** Patients want to ask questions and share experiences, not just receive monologues. So, post conversation-starters: e.g., "What worries you most about your knee pain?" Then respond to each comment. A doctor who started asking questions on Facebook and replied personally doubled their followers in weeks. Take Action: This week, post one open question on your clinic's page and respond warmly to every answer. Notice how this builds goodwill and insight into patient concerns.

Platform Spotlight: Where to Connect

No one platform does it all. Focus on a mix that matches your patients:

- **Your Website & Google Business:** Treat your website as a friendly "online clinic." Make it mobile-friendly and include clear info: your specialties, address, hours, and a friendly photo. Start a blog or FAQ page: even a post answering "What to expect in a diabetes check-up" boosts SEO and helps patients. Complete your Google Business Profile – add a smiling photo of yourself and the clinic. Google research shows complete profiles get *five times* more views. Claim your spot on Google Maps, and keep all info up-to-date. Think local: add your clinic to directories like Practo, Lybrate, or local chamber sites. Even listing opening hours and fees consistently (Google and Practo should match) builds trust.

- **Online Reviews:** Word-of-mouth has gone digital. About **84–94% of patients** check reviews when choosing a doctor. After a positive visit, gently invite satisfied patients to leave an honest review on Google or Facebook (a business card with a link helps). Aim for *authentic* feedback – a few 4-star reviews mixed in with 5-star reviews actually look more credible than all 5-stars. Always **respond** to reviews (even a "Thank you" suffices) – research shows 65% of people value doctors who reply, as it shows you care. If a negative review appears, stay professional: apologise for the experience and invite the person to discuss offline. Never fake reviews – that breaches trust and the rules.
- **Social media (Facebook, Instagram, LinkedIn, YouTube):** Choose 1–2 platforms your patients use. (e.g., older patients: Facebook; young parents: Instagram.) Post short, helpful content regularly. Ideas: infographics on health tips ("5 ways to lower BP"), myth-busters ("Vaccine facts"), or simple how-to videos ("What to do for a sprained ankle"). Apollo Hospitals' Facebook Live Q&A sessions are a great model – specialists answer patient questions in real time, boosting engagement and trust. Even quick videos (the "Mayo Clinic Minute" is famous in the US) get

shared. Remember: **Don't give specific medical advice to non-patients** online; keep it general and educational, and always encourage in-person consultation for personal issues.

- **WhatsApp:** In India, WhatsApp is everywhere. Use a dedicated WhatsApp Business number for your clinic. You can send appointment reminders, check-in messages, or health tips (with patient consent) via broadcast lists or groups. For example, Dr. Kamath in Karnataka runs a "Cardiology at Doorsteps" WhatsApp group for rural patients, sharing tips and even reviewing ECGs – a non-commercial support service that built huge trust. You might start a small group for your diabetic patients, sending monthly blood-sugar check reminders, or broadcast a seasonal health tip ("Flu season is here – get your shot!"). Always let people opt in and out, and keep messages brief and valuable.
- **Email Newsletters:** If you collect emails (with consent), send a monthly newsletter. A short "Tip of the Month" on sleep, diet, or exercise, plus a clinic update, can keep you in your patients' minds. Even a 20% open rate means many are reading your advice. Tools like Mailchimp or your clinic software can automate this.
- **Video and Blogging:** If you're comfortable, start a YouTube channel or blog. A 3-minute chat (phone camera is fine) on a common issue ("Heart-healthy diet basics") can reach far. Patients hear your voice and see your face, which humanizes you. Even an FAQ column ("FAQ Fridays") on your website blog can do wonders. Always cite reputable sources (WHO, national health sites) if you quote stats, which boosts credibility.

Action Plan

1. **Listen to Your Patients:** Survey or simply ask current patients which platforms they use and what they want to learn. This guides your content choice. For example, if many elderly patients rely on Facebook, prioritise a Facebook page.
2. **Set Up Your Digital Hub:** Complete your Google Business Profile and clinic website. Post a welcome note or FAQs on your site. Verify your address/hours on Google.
3. **Encourage Reviews Ethically:** After visits, say: "If you have a moment, please share your feedback on Google – it helps us improve." Provide a link or card (no incentives!). Then, acknowledge reviews promptly.
4. **Create a Content Calendar:** Plan one piece of content per week or month. Choose topics from common patient questions. Use simple tools (smartphone, Canva) to create. Share across channels: blog, social media, WhatsApp.
5. **Engage Actively:** Reply to every comment or message. Host occasional live Q&A (announce it in advance). Personal interactions online create loyal followers.
6. **Leverage Patient Stories:** With consent, share anonymized success stories in your newsletter or on social media. ("After 5 years of migraines, Mr. B reduced headaches by 80% following our plan. We're proud of his progress!")
7. **Stay Ethical and Compliant:** Keep marketing within the rules. Always have written consent for stories, disclose any affiliations, and never spam. Treat your online interactions as an extension of the trust you build in person.

Some Inspiring Examples to Get You Motivated & Started!

- **Apollo Hospitals' Facebook Live** sessions dramatically increased engagement and trust.
- **Mayo Clinic's short, patient-friendly videos** have millions of views.
- **Locally, a Jaipur dentist uses Instagram to demystify dental care** with weekly tips, and saw many patients mention these videos in their appointments.

These examples show that *compassionate, consistent, authentic content* brings new patients and turns existing ones into advocates.

Your Go-To Branding Checklist

Before moving on, make sure to integrate these branding basics:

- ☑ Do I have a complete Google Business profile (photo, hours, etc.)?
- ☑ Is my clinic listed correctly on major directories (Google Maps, Practo, Lybrate)?
- ☑ Do I post patient-first content (tips, FAQs) at least once a month?
- ☑ Have I responded to every recent review?
- ☑ Do I have a simple schedule for updating my profiles and posting content?

By following this roadmap, you'll build an online presence that feels like a friendly, helpful clinic waiting room. Remember: the goal isn't to advertise, but to **extend your patient-first care into every digital channel**. Over time, a strong, trustworthy brand will draw patients to you – because you're meeting them where they're already looking for help.

CHAPTER 3

Building a Thriving Practice: Systems, Not Stress

"Great care doesn't happen by chance — it happens by design. Systems don't replace your compassion; they protect it."

If you've ever left a clinic day thinking, **"I didn't even have time to breathe,"** you're not alone. Physicians are trained to heal, not to run businesses, and the result can be relentless overwork and burnout. But **"Systems, not stress,"** can be your mantra. By designing clear systems and routines for your practice, you turn chaos into order. Instead of firefighting, you'll work proactively. When well-designed processes handle the routine burdens, you can focus on what you do best: caring for patients.

Why Systems Matter

Imagine sailing a ship without a rudder, constant steering, course-correcting, and exhaustion. **Many doctors respond to growing workloads by simply working longer, but sheer willpower isn't sustainable.**

Systems are your invisible helpers: they don't forget steps, don't take breaks, and give your team confidence.

They create breathing room. With good systems, much of your practice runs on "autopilot," not by frantic guessing each day.

This doesn't make care impersonal; it *frees* you to add personal touches because you're not stuck firefighting paperwork.

We'll tackle three critical areas:

1. **Patient Flow:** How patients move through your clinic.
2. **Billing and Finances:** Ensuring steady, error-free revenue.
3. **Compliance and Quality:** Staying audit-ready and building trust.

System for Smart Patient Flow: Make It Predictable

The Problem

Dr. Ananyaa used to joke that her clinic's motto was "Hurry Up and Wait." Mornings started okay, but by noon, a long consult or extra walk-in would throw the whole day off. Her waiting room was filled with frustrated patients, and she skipped lunch trying to catch up. Sound familiar? If so, the good news is: **it can get better**.

Map the Journey

First, define ***patient flow*** – **the journey from "I need a doctor" to "I'm out of the door" and beyond (even follow-ups).** When flow is smooth, waits shrink, mood improves, and patients and providers both feel calm. It's not about squeezing more people in; it's about using time efficiently.

Action Steps

- **Create a Patient Journey Map: List every step:** incoming call, booking, check-in, waiting, consultation, investigations, billing, and follow-up. Identify pain points (e.g., "calls missed" or "double-entry of data").
- **Simplify Scheduling:** Use an appointment software or even a shared Google Calendar. Clearly define slot lengths (e.g., 10 mins for simple cases, 30 mins for new patients). If you allow walk-ins, set a clear quota per day. Always confirm appointments with an automated SMS/WhatsApp reminder the day before, including prep instructions (e.g., "Please come fasting").

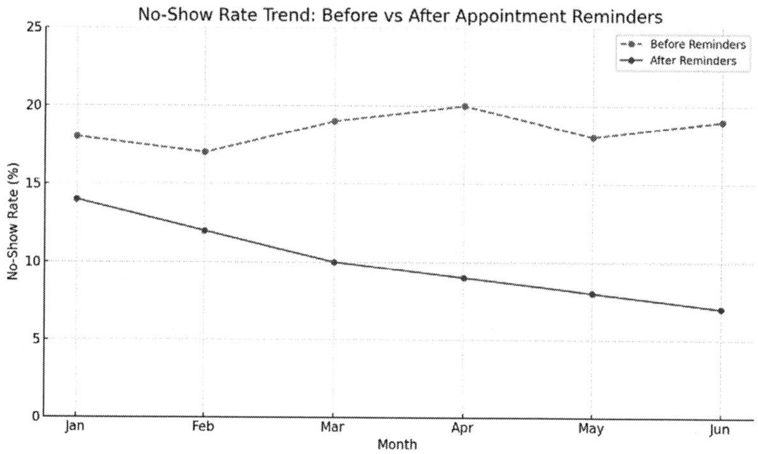

- **Set Realistic Time Slots:** Recognize that some days will have complex cases. Build 10-15 min "buffers" into your schedule or plan a longer consultation at day's start. If a patient is running late, have a policy of informing (e.g., "Last entry by 10 minutes late, we may have to reschedule," posted visibly but said kindly).

- **Front-Desk Protocol:** Train staff on clear steps for check-in: verify patient name/appointment, handle payments if due, and inform the doctor of any special issues. Empower them to manage minor issues: e.g., if labs are pending, staff can bring forms rather than the patient asking you.

Token System and SMS Alerts Reduced Wait Time Significantly

Dr. *Meera Kulkarni (Name Changed), a general physician practicing in **Kothrud, Pune**, was struggling with long patient wait times and growing frustration in her clinic. On most days, her reception area would overflow by mid-morning. Patients often had no idea when their turn would come, leading to repeated interruptions at the front desk and a rushed atmosphere inside the consultation room.

The Challenge

Patients were arriving without clear time slots, especially walk-ins. Although appointments were noted in a register, there was no queue discipline. Staff felt overwhelmed, and Dr. Meera found herself skipping breaks to catch up.

The Solution

In February 2024, Dr. Meera implemented two small but impactful systems:

1. **Digital Token System**: A simple tablet-based token app was installed at reception. Each patient received a token number at check-in, visible on a wall-mounted screen. A small bell and display notified the next number being served.

2. **SMS Alerts**: Patients registering with their phone number received an automatic SMS confirming their token and approximate wait time. If the wait exceeded 30 minutes, they received an update:

   "Dear Mr. Patil, Token #17 is now estimated at 11:20 AM. You can wait in your car or a nearby cafe. We'll notify you 2 tokens before your turn."

The Phenomenal Result

Within **six weeks,**

- **Average wait time dropped by 35%**
- **Fewer front-desk interruptions**
- **Happier patients who appreciated the flexibility**
- **More on-time consultations for Dr. Meera**

Dr. Meera Reflected,

"I thought high-tech systems were only for big hospitals. But this small change gave my patients a sense of respect, and gave me breathing room."

- **Manage Wait Time:** Use numbers or queue boards. Allow patients to wait in a separate lounge or even at home (with a message when their turn is near) if the wait is long. Keep patients informed: "The doctor is running 20 minutes behind today. We apologize; we appreciate your patience."
- **Huddle and Handovers:** Start the day with a 5-minute team briefing. Go over any special cases and clarify roles. End the day with a quick check-in: what worked, what didn't. This communication loop prevents repeated chaos.
- **Continuous Improvement:** Pick one bottleneck each week to fix. For instance, if imaging reports are taking too long, find out why (maybe call your lab for a turnaround commitment). Tiny fixes add up.

System for Seamless Billing and Revenue

Revenue should come predictably, not as a surprise. Many clinics suffer cash-flow gaps or billing errors from ad-hoc methods. Here's how to stabilise finances:

- **Consistent Coding:** Use a standard template or software for recording diagnoses and procedures (e.g., ICD-10 codes, if needed). Train staff to use it properly. Consistency prevents insurance disputes and audit flags.
- **Transparent Pricing:** List fees for common services (consultation, tests, procedures) on your website and reception. This builds trust and avoids "sticker shock." Offer package pricing for common bundles (e.g., "Annual Check-Up Package" including tests at a slight discount).
- **Efficient Billing Process:** Empower front-desk staff with a clear billing workflow. An SOP (Standard Operating Procedure) sheet that walks them through: patient code entry, payment collection, receipt generation, and record updating. Use software, if possible, to reduce manual errors.

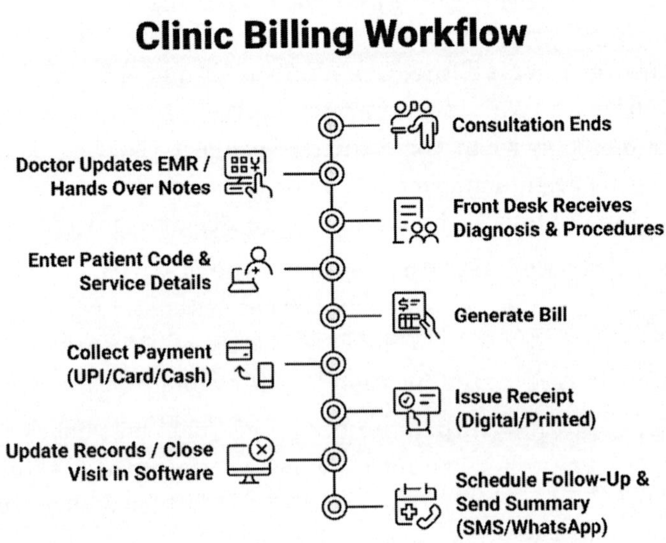

- **Follow-Up on Payments:** If patients owe money (unscheduled tests, long-term care), set reminders (calls or messages) until payment. Offer easy modes: UPI, credit card, and online transfer. For bulk patients (e.g., corporate plans), send monthly statements.
- **Monitor Key Metrics:** Each month, track: total revenue, average revenue per patient, percentage of insurance vs cash, and days sales outstanding (how long before receivables are collected). A simple spreadsheet can flag trends early (e.g., declining revenue or rising uncollected bills).
- **Budget for Growth:** Allocate funds monthly for improvements (new equipment, staff training). Even a small 5% reinvestment fund can finance big changes over a year (e.g., hiring a part-time coordinator).

System for Compliance and Quality

Staying audit-ready protects you legally and builds patient confidence. A sudden inspection of records, or a minor regulatory change, should not upend your day:

- **Standardize Documentation:** Maintain clear, legible, and dated patient records. Use a consistent format: chief complaint, findings, treatment, follow-up plan. If you use any digital tools, ensure they comply with privacy rules.
- **SOPs for Regular Processes:** Have documented protocols for common compliance areas: when to seek consent, how to store waste, how to fire an errant employee, etc. For example, keep the MCI-approved consent forms handy; don't scribble notes on loose paper.
- **Regular Audits:** Once a quarter, review a random sample of files for completeness (signatures, consent, follow-ups noted) and billing accuracy. Check that all required licenses and insurance policies for the clinic are up to date (display renewals where staff can see).

- **Fire Safety & Accessibility:** Ensure fire extinguishers are serviced and visible. Keep entrances and exits clear. (These small checks can save lives and prevent fines.)
- **Team Training:** Conduct a monthly "compliance minute" – cover one topic (e.g., patient confidentiality dos and don'ts) in a brief huddle. Empower staff to flag non-compliance immediately, e.g., "I noticed this patient left without signing consent – let's fix it."

Teamwork and Training

A practice is only as strong as its team. Delegate, train, and trust:

- **Define Roles Clearly:** Everyone should know their responsibilities. Create simple job descriptions (written or illustrated) for front-desk, nursing, billing, etc. Post them in the staff area. This reduces overlap and finger-pointing.
- **Empower Staff:** Let your team solve small problems. For example, authorize receptionists to reschedule appointments if you're unexpectedly tied up, or allow nurses to give common patient education (e.g., diet tips) after a protocol.
- **Regular Meetings:** A short weekly team meeting can address issues before they blow up. Review patient flow hiccups, share patient compliments, and brainstorm improvement ideas.
- **Cross-Training:** Teach staff to cover each other. If the billing clerk is on leave, the receptionist should know the basics of running that process. This reduces panic when someone is absent.
- **Celebrate Successes:** Acknowledge when systems work. Did the new reminder system drop no-shows? Share the good news at a meeting. Positive reinforcement encourages continued use of systems.

Your Systems Action Checklist

- ☑ Map your current workflows for patient flow, billing, and documentation. Identify one 'pain point' in each to address this month.
- ☑ Draft or refine two SOPs (e.g., "Check-in Process" and "End-of-day Cash Reconciliation").
- ☑ Schedule a 5-minute daily meeting with staff to coordinate daily goals.
- ☑ Hold a compliance "check" day: verify licenses, fire extinguishers, and a sample of records.
- ☑ Review your financial dashboard monthly (revenue, expenses, no-shows) to spot trends.

By building these systems, you reduce the daily chaos. You'll find that a well-run practice is not only more profitable but *more compassionate*, because doctors and staff have the mental space to focus on patient care instead of paperwork and firefighting.

CHAPTER 4

LIFELONG LEARNING: STAYING RELEVANT IN MEDICINE

"The best doctors never stop being students, because medicine evolves, and so must we. Learning isn't extra work; it's the work that makes everything easier."

Medicine and healthcare management are moving targets. New treatments emerge, patient expectations shift, and technology evolves. To **stay relevant and thrive**, you need a mindset of continuous learning beyond the stethoscope. This means cultivating non-clinical skills (leadership, finance, digital literacy) alongside your medical expertise.

The Knowledge Economy in Healthcare

Being a brilliant diagnostician no longer guarantees practice growth.

Today's patients compare clinics as much on convenience, communication, and digital savvy as on clinical outcomes.

For instance, around **77% of patients now search online before booking a doctor.**

If your practice lacks a website, online reviews, or appointment reminders, many patients might not even discover you. Moreover, **80% of patients say they prefer digital communication (emails, texts) for routine reminders.** In short, healthcare is increasingly run like a service industry.

If you don't learn business and tech skills, competitors will. Doctors who adapt by improving their online presence or workflow often *reverse declines* in referrals and attract new patients. Consider this: one study showed that clinics with an active social media page saw patient inquiries double compared to those without.

Auditing Your Skills and Setting Goals Personal Skills Audit

Start by honestly rating yourself. Make a list of non-clinical domains: leadership, team management, financial planning, marketing, legal/compliance, tech tools, etc. Rate each from 1 (no experience) to 5 (expert) based on your comfort. Identify your three lowest scores as priorities for growth.

Setting SMART Goals: Once you've chosen a skill to improve, make it SMART (Specific, Measurable, Achievable, Relevant, Time-bound).

For example:

- ***Specific:*** "Complete a 4-week course on Google Business optimization."
- ***Measurable:*** "Increase my clinic's Google inquiries by 50%."
- ***Achievable:*** "Study 30 minutes daily."

- ***Relevant:*** "Supports my goal of growing urban patient visits."
- ***Time-bound:*** "By September 30th."

Write these down. This anchors your learning plan.

SMART Goals Template: Google Business Optimization

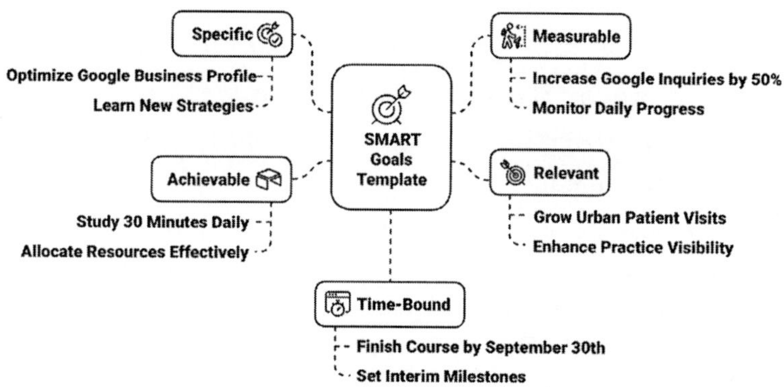

Microlearning & Just-in-Time Training

Busy doctors need bite-sized learning:

- **Podcasts & Webinars:** Subscribe to a few healthcare business podcasts or webinars (IMA leadership series, digital health forums). Listen during commutes or between appointments. Even 10–15 minutes a day adds up.
- **Quick Videos:** Follow channels on YouTube or LinkedIn Learning that offer short (1-5 min) tutorials on leadership, negotiation, or practice management. For instance, a 5-min video on "How to handle difficult patients" can be more useful than an hour-long lecture.
- **Daily Habit:** Block 10–15 minutes in your calendar labelled "Learning – DO NOT INTERRUPT." Treat it like a patient appointment you can't skip. Use that time to read

a summary of a new guideline, watch an educational video, or read a chapter of a healthcare management book.

Formal & Informal Certifications

Consider formal courses for deeper learning:

- **Short Courses:** Platforms like Coursera, Udemy, or edX offer bite-sized courses:
    - **Leadership:** *"Managing Healthcare Teams"*
    - **Finance:** *"Basics of Clinic Accounting"*
    - **Branding/Marketing:** *"Personal Brand for Professionals"*
- **Certifications:** Traditional CME credits fulfill licensure but often focus clinically. Look at diplomas or certificates in Hospital/Health Administration, Quality Management, or Digital Health. Even a 6-week online program can give you frameworks for practice growth.

Peer Learning & Mastermind Groups

You don't have to go it alone:

- **Start a Cohort:** Invite 3–5 doctor friends or colleagues to form a peer group. Meet fortnightly (Zoom or in person). Each session, one member presents a challenge (e.g., "My appointment system is chaotic") and the group brainstorms solutions. Rotate the presenter.
- **Accountability:** Set shared goals. For example, "By our next meeting, try a new scheduling app." Discuss what worked or didn't. This accountability keeps you committed.
- **Benefits:** You gain diverse perspectives and support. A surgeon might have marketing tips, while a pediatrician offers team-training hacks. Sharing lessons means you learn faster than alone.

Conferences, Workshops & Retreats

Be strategic about events:

- **Choosing Events:** Look for events that mix theory with practice. IMA leadership summits, hospital management conferences, and digital health expos are great for networking and practical insights.
- **Maximising ROI:** Don't just attend – *prepare and follow up*. Before a conference, set 2–3 objectives (e.g., "Meet one potential referral partner", "Learn about telemedicine billing"). During sessions, take succinct notes and gather contact info. After returning, implement one new idea quickly (maybe a tip on patient app integration). Even a small change keeps your growth momentum.

Keeping Up with Tech & Trends

Technology is constantly evolving, but you can keep pace with minimal effort:

- **Newsletters & Summaries:** Subscribe to one health-tech newsletter (e.g., MedTech Dive, 91mobiles Health) and one healthcare business blog. Skim headlines weekly for relevant trends (e.g., a new health app or government policy).
- **Sandbox Testing:** Set aside a "lab hour" monthly. Experiment with one new tool: install a free EMR trial, try a teleconsultation app, or use an online survey for patient feedback. Evaluate: Is it user-friendly? Does it save time or money? If it passes the test, plan a pilot in your clinic.
- **Peer Recommendations:** Ask fellow doctors which tools they love. Word-of-mouth among colleagues can point you to hidden gems (like a great appointment app one of them developed with an engineer friend).

Your 30-Day Action Plan t

Make learning a habit. Here's a sample first-30-day plan:

- **Week 1:** Complete your skills audit and set one SMART goal. (Write it down.)
- **Week 2:** Block 15 minutes daily in your schedule for microlearning. Invite or join a peer group.
- **Week 3:** Enroll in one short online course aligned to your goal. Subscribe to two relevant newsletters or blogs.
- **Week 4:** Watch one webinar or listen to three podcast episodes on a focus topic. Test one new digital tool in sandbox mode (e.g., set up a demo telehealth account).

By the end of the month, you'll have launched a learning habit. Keep iterating: set a new goal, swap in fresh resources, and celebrate each milestone.

Key Takeaway

- Lifelong learning isn't optional; it's the engine of a thriving career.
- By intentionally growing your non-clinical skills and integrating learning into your routine, you future-proof your practice.
- Each new skill or insight can improve patient care and your bottom line.
- **And remember:** curiosity and humility are as important as any medical degree – stay open to what your patients and peers can teach you.

CHAPTER 5

Ethical Digital Presence: Earning Trust Online

> ***"Your online presence is your new waiting room — clean, clear, and caring. Show up with honesty, and patients will find you even before they meet you."***

Your **online reputation** is now an essential part of your practice.

Patients often "meet" you online before they even step into the clinic.

Statistics back this up: **over 70% of patients search for providers online before booking a visit, and about 84–94%** consult online reviews when choosing a doctor. In India, a Times of India blog noted that people "across the length and breadth" use Google to find doctors. Think of your Google Business listing, Practo profile, and social media as a 24/7 front desk. If your "receptionist" (your online presence) looks incomplete or out-of-date, patients may simply go elsewhere.

Navigating Regulations and Ethics

India's medical councils are strict: advertising is largely forbidden. You can share facts (specialty, qualifications, location), but *not* promotional claims or guaranteed outcomes. For instance, the Maharashtra Medical Council warns against any social media post promising "100% cure" or using patient testimonials as ads.

Always lead with service, not sales. In practice:

- Avoid superlatives ("best hospital in the city").
- Don't share patient photos or stories without written consent.
- Stick to educational content ("What does high BP mean?") rather than offers.
- Disclose any affiliations (e.g., "I serve on a committee at XYZ hospital").

By staying within these guidelines, you not only protect your license but also build genuine patient trust.

Claiming and Optimizing Your Online Presence

Google Business Profile (GBP): Start by "claiming" your listing. **Make sure every field is filled:** address,

- **Phone**
- **Business Hours**
- **Website,**
- **And a photo of yourself (preferably in a white coat).**

A complete GBP gets *five times* more views.

> A doctor in Patna, who fully optimized her profile (**added photos, Hindi language option, responded to reviews**), **saw a 20% jump in new patients.**

Add a brief welcome message or your mission ("Caring for Bengaluru's smiles since 2005") and update any seasonal changes (extra Sunday hours, Diwali closure, etc.).

Practices, Websites, and Blogs: If you have a site, make it patient-friendly:

- **About Page:** Share your story and approach. A personal photo with your team adds warmth.
- **Services and Fees:** Clearly list what you offer (e.g., "Home visits, Teleconsultations, IVF services") and any standard charges. Transparency here builds confidence.
- **Blog/FAQ:** Regularly post helpful articles: "Managing monsoon illnesses", "Guide to prenatal checkups", etc. Even short, 300-word posts boost SEO and patient trust. You don't need fancy writing; just answer the common questions you hear daily.
- **Multilingual Content:** If you serve regional populations, consider adding content in local languages. For example, an ophthalmologist in Tamil Nadu might post "கண் பரிசோதனை இளஞ்சிறதனா?" (What happens during an eye check-up?) for Tamil-speaking patients.

> An Ahmedabad cardiologist **started posting weekly heart-health tips in English and Gujarati** on his website. Patients told him later **they felt more connected to the practice because the content was in their language.)**

Managing Reviews and Feedback

Reviews are powerful social proof.

Politely encourage happy patients to leave reviews. Don't force anyone, though.

- **After a successful visit, say:** "We value your feedback! If you can spare a minute, please share your honest review on Google". Handing a card with a short URL can help.
- **Emphasize honesty:** "Whether it's a compliment or a suggestion, it helps us serve you better." Research suggests a mix of 4- and 5-star reviews looks more genuine than a wall of 5 stars.
- **Respond Quickly:** Every review deserves a response. For a positive review: "Thank you, Mr. Sharma! So glad you appreciated our care" builds rapport. For a negative review: apologize for their experience and invite them to discuss offline ("I'm sorry to hear this, please call us so we can address your concern"). Never argue publicly or reveal any private info.
- **Goal-Set:** Aim for small, steady goals: e.g., "Gain 5 new Google reviews by next quarter." Track which platform (Google, Practo, Facebook) yields the most visibility for you.

Over time, an active presence of reviews and replies will reassure new patients. They see you *listening* and improving.

Building Patient-First Online Content

Drawing from Chapter 2's principles, frame your social media posts as education:

- **Health Tips:** "5 ways to prevent common cold", "Importance of hydration in summer", etc. Short bullets or infographics work well.

- **Myth Busters:** Tackle misconceptions ("Myth: Vaccines cause illness. Fact: Vaccines train the immune system safely").
- **Celebrate Health Days:** On World Diabetes Day, post a simple chart on managing sugar; on Heart Day, share an exercise video.
- **Interactive Posts:** Ask questions ("What worries you about knee pain?"), run polls (LinkedIn/Facebook polls on topics), or host "ask the doctor" sessions where patients submit queries.

For each post, use plain language as if talking to a friend. Avoid advertising language. If you do share a case story, *anonymize it fully* and focus on what patients learned. Example: "A 50-year-old man came in with persistent heartburn. After tests, we found it was due to [common cause]. With lifestyle changes and medicine, he's much better now – something that many can relate to." Then allow comments or DMs for questions.

> **A Bangalore pediatrician began weekly Facebook Live sessions answering parents' questions** (e.g., on childhood nutrition). After a few months, **many parents started mentioning these videos when booking appointments.** It became both a service and a soft brand-building tool.

WhatsApp Groups & Newsletters: As mentioned, consider small opt-in groups: e.g., a WhatsApp group for diabetic patients where you share a "tip of the week". Or a monthly email with a "health tip + patient story" (Mailchimp or even a simple PDF) – doctors have seen open rates of 20–30% with useful content.

Always be sincere and helpful. The more your online voice sounds like *you in person*, the more patients will trust that it's an extension of the care you provide in the clinic.

Monitor, Measure, and Improve

- **Audit Yourself:** Every quarter, Google your own name and clinic. See what comes up. If an outdated directory shows wrong hours, update or remove it.
- **Google Alerts:** Set alerts for your name or clinic. You'll get an email if anyone mentions you online.
- **Analytics:** If your website has Google Analytics or similar, check traffic: what pages are popular? Which posts do readers click? If you post on social media, note engagement (likes, comments, shares). Use these metrics to refine content.
- **Team Discussion:** In monthly staff meetings, share social media highlights and ask: "What patient questions do we still need content for?" If patients keep asking the same question, make a post about it.
- **Iterate:** Your online presence should evolve. As you learn what resonates, do more of that. If a format (video, infographic, blog) flops, try something else.

Reputation Metrics Comparison

	Page Visits	Patient Reviews	Social Followers
Jan	350	12 ★★★★★	800
Feb	470	15 ★★★★☆	950
Mar	620	20 ★★★★★	1200

Key Takeaway

- In the digital age, building trust means being a reliable source in the online spaces your patients use.
- By carefully curating your online presence, respecting ethics, sharing knowledge, and engaging, your digital footprint will support and extend your practice.
- It's not extra work; it's part of modern patient care.

CHAPTER 6

SETTING UP OPERATIONS THAT SCALE: YOUR THIRD STEP

> ***"Technology doesn't have to be flashy or futuristic to be powerful. Sometimes, the simplest tools – your phone, a reminder app, or a short video – can quietly revolutionize your care."***

When we say "technology," many doctors imagine MRI machines or robots.

Instead, think small:

- Your smartphone,
- Simple Apps,
- And automations that save time and stress.

The aim is **"working smarter, not harder"** with tech that fits your coat pocket, not just your lab coat pocket.

A Mindset Shift: Tools for Time Freedom

You don't need a crore-dollar investment to transform your practice. A few examples:

- **Electronic Health Records (EHR/EMR):** Even a basic cloud-based app that stores patient history can make follow-ups easier. Imagine a patient walks in: instead of asking, "Have we met before?", you glance at the app: *"Ah, Mr. Sharma – BP follow-up from July 2022. How's your medication?"* That instant recall (and trust-building) comes from simple record-keeping.
- **Auto-Reminders:** Set up an SMS or WhatsApp system to ping patients before appointments or due follow-ups. A gentle automated message ("Mr. Sharma, your check-up is due next week, please call to schedule") can yield bookings without staff effort.
- **Educational Videos:** If you find yourself explaining the same exercises or post-op care repeatedly (**as Dr. Raghav did in a tier-2 city**), simply record one clear video. Send that video via WhatsApp to patients after their surgery. It builds consistency in your care, even if you're not physically repeating yourself. This took Dr. Raghav *no* tech course or big budget – just his smartphone and a bit of time.

Clinic Apps and Electronic Records

- **Choosing an EMR:** If you see many repeat patients or manage chronic cases, even a simple EMR can help. Look for user-friendly ones used by Indian clinics (like *Medibuddy Ray, KareXpert, or Lybrate EMR*). Key features: easy data entry, offline access (for areas with patchy internet), and the ability to print or message summaries. Begin with the basics: create one profile per patient with their visit history.
- **Templates:** Customize templates within your EMR: common prescriptions, referral letters, and follow-up instructions. This saves time and ensures consistency. For example, a cardiologist might have a template for "antihypertensive routine counseling".

Automation and Reminders

- **Appointment Reminders:** Most practice management software includes auto-reminders. If you're not ready for software, even WhatsApp Business has Quick Replies and Broadcast Lists. You can save quick-reply texts like: "Confirming your 10 AM slot on Tue. Reply *YES* to confirm". Just a one-time setup can automate dozens of daily messages.
- **Birthdays and Health Check Reminders:** Keep patients engaged by remembering them. A simple script can flag upcoming birthdays (or anniversaries), and your system can send a greeting (manual or automated). Or use it to remind pregnant patients of their next antenatal visit dates.

Telehealth and Virtual Care

The pandemic fast-tracked telemedicine in India, and it's here to stay. Even small investments (a good internet connection and a private WhatsApp video or Zoom account) allow:

- **Follow-up Calls:** Instead of "urgent" visits for routine updates, schedule teleconsults. Patients love the convenience, and it frees clinic slots.
- **Telemedicine Apps:** Platforms like Practo, MFine, or government portals (eSanjeevani) are becoming popular. Joining one can expand your reach to remote patients.

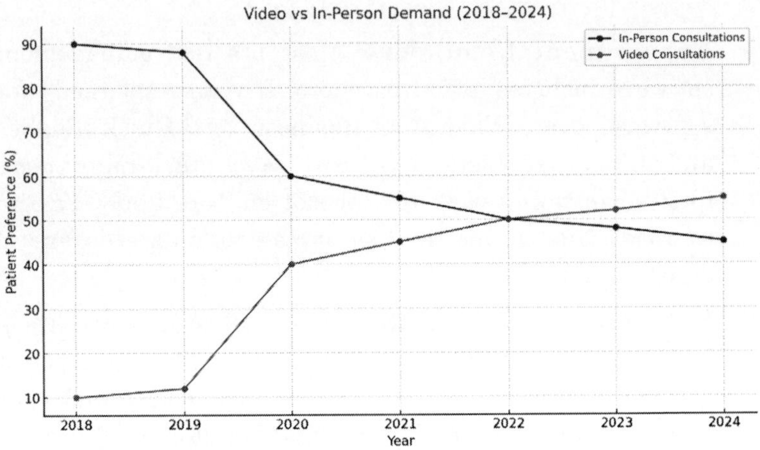

- **Digital Monitoring:** For chronic care, simple home-monitoring devices (BP cuff, glucometer) plus photo or app sharing of readings can keep you informed. Ask patients to message you their results weekly for adjustments.

Data and AI — What's Realistic Today

Don't be overwhelmed by talk of AI. Right now, AI in most clinics is basic:

- **Smartphone Apps:** Spell-check on prescription texts, voice-to-text for notes, and even some medication-interaction checkers on apps.
- **Decision Support:** A few EMRs offer drug interaction alerts or risk calculators.
- **Data Visualization:** If you collect patient data (say, monthly blood sugar logs), simple Excel or Google Sheets can chart progress and flag trends.

Focus on adoption over innovation. The most powerful tech improvements in many clinics came from *doctors using simple tools consistently*:

- A physician who set up auto-reminders halved his missed appointments.
- Clinics using an EMR reported more complete records and easier audits.
- Doctors who asked patients to follow their Facebook/ Instagram health tips saw a 30% increase in walk-ins from new patients.

Your Action Toolkit

- **Evaluate one aspect of your workflow today:** could a simple app or tool help? (E.g., patient check-in, prescription printing, file backups?) Research one or two and try a demo.
- **Consolidate tech:** Use WhatsApp Business for clinic use (keep personal and work separate).
- **Involve your team:** Assign one staff member as a "tech champion" to explore and train others on any new tool.
- **Stay Safe:** Ensure any patient data on devices is password-protected and backed up.

Embracing these ground-level tech tools means **less time chasing forms and more time being a doctor**. You don't have to become an IT expert—just a little tech-aware and curious. Each small tech adoption is a step toward a more efficient, modern practice and a more connected, empowered you.

CHAPTER 7

PATIENT ENGAGEMENT: CONNECTING BEYOND CARE

"Medicine is not just about curing illness, but about building relationships that heal. An engaged patient isn't just treated— they're empowered."

Building a successful practice is not a one-time transaction; it's an ongoing relationship.

Patient engagement means involving patients in their own health, educating them, and ensuring they feel part of the care team. Engaged patients adhere better to treatment and become your advocates.

Beyond the Transaction

Engagement begins **even before** clinical interaction. Think of patients as partners. A patient who is informed about their condition and involved in decision-making is more likely to trust you and follow your advice. Simple tactics:

- **Shared Decision-Making:** When presenting options (say, surgery vs. physiotherapy), invite the patient's input:

"What concerns you most about these choices?" Respect their preferences.

- **Accessible Materials:** Have brochures or digital handouts on common conditions that patients can take home. For example, a pamphlet on migraine triggers or a table of normal blood sugar values can empower patients to manage at home.

Health Education and Empowerment

Make education a part of every visit and beyond:

- **In-Clinic Materials:** Posters, models, or video loops in waiting areas on topics like hand-washing, healthy cooking, or warning signs.

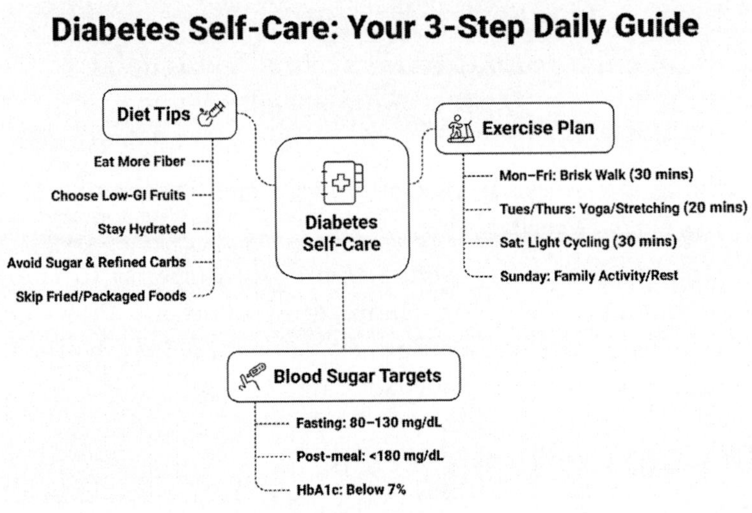

- **Workshops and Classes:** Organize occasional free talks or group sessions. For example, a quarterly "Parents' Seminar" on childhood vaccinations, or a weekly free yoga/diabetes clinic at your center. These positions place you as a community educator and let patients interact.

- **Chronic Care Programs:** For patients with chronic diseases (diabetes, hypertension), create a mini "program": scheduled check-ins, a simple logbook, or a WhatsApp group for tips. Example: A group of hypertensive patients might meet monthly for BP checks and Q&A with you.

Building Long-Term Relationships

- **Personal Touches:** Remember details about your patients. Note family names or work stressors in records, and ask about them on your next visit ("How's your son's surgery going?"). This shows genuine care.
- **Follow-Up Communication:** A quick call or message a week after treatment to check progress can make patients feel seen. For instance, "Mr. Iyer, I hope your knee is feeling better. How are you doing with the exercises?" Often, just this care reminder prevents complications and deepens trust.
- **Patient Portals:** If you have an EMR or simple app, consider giving patients access to their records and test results. This transparency engages them (they can see lab reports as soon as they arrive) and reduces phone calls for updates.

Community Outreach and Support

Expand engagement beyond the clinic walls:

- **Health Camps:** Partner with local NGOs or pharma companies (ethically and informatively) to host health camps. For instance, a free eye-checkup camp at a local school or community center. It helps those in need and spreads your name through service.
- **School and Corporate Talks:** Offer to speak at nearby schools on topics like hygiene, first-aid, or nutrition. For

local businesses, conduct wellness sessions ("Desk Yoga for office workers") – this positions you as a caring expert in the community.

- **Patient Advisory Group:** Invite a few representative patients (with diverse backgrounds) to meet once a quarter for feedback. Ask: "How can we serve you better?" Their insights (e.g., "We wish appointment booking were easier" or "More evening slots are needed") can guide improvements you might not have considered.

Listening to Patient Feedback

In every interaction, remember: Every touchpoint is an opportunity. From the receptionist's smile to the clarity of your prescription note – these shape loyalty. Strategies include:

- **Suggestion Box:** Physical or digital (anonymized). Periodically say, "We welcome any feedback about your experience here."
- **Patient Surveys:** Quick forms with 2-3 questions can yield insights. Keep them short and anonymous.
- **Feedback Loop:** Show patients you acted on their input (poster or email: "We heard your feedback. Our lab now opens at 8 AM for early appointments."). This reinforces engagement.

> A pediatric clinic in Mumbai created a "Young Parents Club." Every month, families with infants were invited for a group session led by the pediatrician on topics like breastfeeding or immunizations. Parents appreciated the support and became fiercely loyal, often referring friends.

Key Takeaway

Engaged patients become your partners in health and your biggest advocates. By educating, involving, and listening to them, you create a culture of care that goes beyond the prescription pad. Engagement boosts outcomes (patients stick to treatment), satisfaction (they feel valued), and growth (they recommend you).

(Figure suggestion: **Patient Engagement Funnel:** a flowchart from "First Visit" to "Long-term Care Plan" highlighting touchpoints like education, follow-ups, and support groups.)*

CHAPTER 8

Platforms to Connect: Online & Offline Strategies

> ***"Today's patient doesn't just walk into your clinic—they Google you, message you, follow you, and then decide. Visibility isn't vanity — it's trust."***

By now, I'm sure you're convinced of the importance of being present **everywhere your patients are looking**. This chapter details the key platforms—both digital and in-person—that doctors can leverage to connect with patients in India.

Google Business Profile (Online)

Why it matters: Google is king in India. When someone searches "orthopedic doctor near me," Google shows local listings first. A **Google Business Profile (GBP)** acts as your clinic's billboard on search results and maps. A complete profile (photos, hours, menu of services) can get five times more clicks than an incomplete one.

Pro Tips:

- Claim and verify your clinic's GBP at google.com/business. Add high-quality photos: exterior, waiting area, your team at work (with patient permission), and any certifications displayed on walls.
- Enable messaging on GBP so patients can text you directly through the listing.
- Respond to Google messages quickly (people expect fast replies).
- **Avoid pitfalls:** Don't leave any field blank (like working hours), and never use promotional language in your business name. If you move or change hours, update Google immediately. Merge any duplicate listings (one listing per clinic location and doctor role) to avoid confusion.

Practo and Other Directories (Online)

Why it matters: In India, many still trust platforms like Practo for finding doctors and booking appointments. Practo is also a software platform; 120,000+ doctors use it. Being active here puts you in front of digitally-minded patients.

Pro Tips:

- Create a detailed Practo profile: specialties, qualifications, photos, and fees. Patients often book directly through Practo.
- Use Practo's practice management tools if useful (it can manage appointments and reminders).
- Keep it updated: wrong info (phone number, timings) on Practo frustrates patients.
- Respond to Practo appointment requests promptly (the system flags if you ignore them).

- **Avoid Pitfall:** Be wary of scam calls claiming to help with listings – only trust known sources.

WhatsApp Business (Online)

Why it matters: WhatsApp has ~600 million users in India, making it an unparalleled communication channel. The WhatsApp Business app provides features to separate personal and business communication.

Pro Tips:

- **Dedicated Number:** Use a clinic-only number. Never mix your private chats with patient chats.
- **Quick Replies:** Pre-save common replies. E.g., "Hi! This is Dr. Kapoor's clinic. To book an appointment, reply with *APPT*." This can save time during busy times.
- **Appointment Scheduling:** Let patients schedule by messaging. It's fast and many prefer it over calls.
- **Reminders and Follow-ups:** Use the broadcast feature to send reminders or health tips to patients who opt in. ("Reminder: Annual check-up due. Call us to schedule.")
- **Medical Advice:** Strictly limit medical advice to general tips. Use WhatsApp for logistics and education only, never for detailed consultations (especially emergency issues). Encourage patients to come to the clinic for anything serious.
- **Privacy:** Always get explicit consent before adding patients to any broadcast list. If someone marks your messages as spam, your account could be blocked.
- **Avoid Pitfall:** Don't ignore WhatsApp queries for days – patients expect rapid replies. If you're away, use the automated away message to manage expectations.

Social Media: Facebook & Instagram (Online)

Why it matters: Over 500 million Indians use social media, including many patients and their families. Facebook has a broad reach; Instagram is great for visual engagement (especially with younger audiences).

Pro Tips:

- **Page/Profile:** Create a Facebook Page for your clinic and an Instagram business account. Use your practice or doctor photo and logo for profile pics.
- **Content Strategy:** Post regularly (1–2 times a week) with a mix of:
  - **Tips & Education:** Infographics on health tips (hydration, exercise), short videos answering FAQs.
  - **Behind-the-Scenes:** Introduce your team. A photo of your nurse explaining a procedure (with patient consent) can highlight care quality.
  - **Patient Stories:** With permission, share anonymized success stories ("Met Mr. Rao today, who improved his breathing after our asthma plan!").
  - **Community Involvement:** Share photos from a recent health camp or a group photo at a conference you attended. This shows leadership.
- **Engagement:** Encourage sharing. E.g., "Tag a friend who would benefit from these tips." Run Q&As or polls ("Which topic should I cover next?").
- **Tools:** Use Canva or a similar tool to make appealing graphics. Even a smartphone camera can take decent photos in a clinic setting.

Dr. Sharma, a Jaipur dentist, uses Instagram Stories to post quick dental health tips daily and posts patient smile transformations (before/after with consent).

His followers have grown, and many bookings now mention an Instagram post they saw.

YouTube and Video Content (Online)

Why it matters: Video builds trust faster than text. A YouTube channel (or even posting on Facebook/Instagram) with short educational clips can position you as an expert.

Pro Tips:

- **Start Simple:** Even your phone camera is enough. Focus on steady framing and good lighting (sit facing a window if possible).
- **Content Ideas:** "A day in the life of a GP", "3 ways to lower cholesterol", demo how to change a dressing, or myth vs. fact segments.
- **Titling:** Use clear titles with common terms ("Knee Pain Relief Exercises"). This helps patients find you. Add subtitles for clarity if possible.
- **Consistency:** Regularly upload (e.g., one short video per month). Share the video link on your social channels.

Offline Platforms: Health Camps, Talks, Local Media

Being present offline still matters greatly in India, as already discussed in the previous chapter, too. Here are some great ways to build your offline presence and impact:

- **Health Camps:** Organize or participate in free camps in your area (e.g., school vision screenings, village health fairs). These put your name out there and serve the community. Even if not directly profitable, they often lead to long-term patient trust.

- **School/College Talks:** Offer to give talks on hygiene, career advice to med aspirants, or first aid to local schools/ colleges. It's a public service, and it builds your reputation as a caring physician.
- **Corporate Wellness:** Local businesses often invite health professionals to give lunch-time health talks ("Preventing Back Pain in Desk Workers") – this also networks you with potential new patients.
- **Pharmacy & Hospital Networks:** Get to know local pharmacists and smaller clinics; they often refer patients. Providing them with simple referral pads or your cards helps.

Media and Public Relations

- **Local Press:** For any significant event (opening a new branch, launching a free clinic day), send a press release to local newspapers or TV stations. A human-interest angle works well ("Rural Clinic Offers Teleconsultations for Tribal Villages").
- **Interviews:** If you have expertise (e.g., a rare specialty), offer to be a quoted expert for health articles. Even a short quote can get your name in front of thousands.
- **Radio & Podcasts:** Participate in local radio health shows or start a small podcast. Discuss common health topics or health news.

Your Connection & Impact Checklist

- ☑ Have I claimed/updated all online profiles (Google, Practo, etc.)?
- ☑ Is my Facebook/Instagram page updated with recent content (at least monthly)?
- ☑ Have I responded to all patient inquiries on these platforms within 24 hours?
- ☑ Do I have any scheduled offline outreach activities (camps, talks) this quarter?
- ☑ Am I tracking which platforms bring new patient inquiries?

By diversifying your presence across these platforms, you **meet patients wherever they are** – online or offline. Consistency is key: patients trust doctors who are active, responsive, and clearly present. When each channel reflects the same caring message, your overall reach multiplies.

CHAPTER 9

The Business of Healing: Finances & Growth

"Medicine is a calling, but your clinic is a business. Managing your finances well isn't greed – it's responsibility."

Thriving practices are also sound businesses.

Managing finances ethically and strategically ensures you can keep serving patients long-term.

In India today, many physicians overlook this side of medicine, but even simple financial acumen can transform your practice from breaking even to flourishing.

Budgeting and Cash Flow

- **Track Income and Expenses:** Maintain a basic ledger (Excel or accounting software). Record all incoming revenue (consult fees, tests, pharmacy sales) and all expenses (rent, utilities, staff salaries, supplies). Review this monthly.
- **Categorize:** Break expenses into fixed (rent, salaries) and variable (lab reagents, printing pamphlets) costs. Knowing this helps during lean months; you'll see which costs you can trim if needed.

- **Set Budgets:** At the start of each year, allocate budgets for each category (e.g., ₹15,000/month for lab supplies, ₹10,000 for marketing). Aim to keep expenses below 90% of income, leaving a buffer for unexpected costs.
- **Reserve Fund:** Try to maintain at least 2-3 months' worth of expenses in a reserve account. This is your safety net (for equipment repairs, slower seasons, or personal emergencies).

Pricing Services Ethically

- **Transparent Fee Structure:** List fees for common services (consultation, injections, dressing) in reception and/or on your website. This transparency builds trust.
- **Fair Discounts/Packages:** It's okay to offer loyalty discounts (e.g., a 10% discount on a package of 5 physiotherapy sessions) as long as it's not false advertising. Ensure such offers comply with ethical codes.
- **Avoid Overpricing:** Pricing should reflect quality, but also local standards. Overcharging will drive patients away or lead to bad reviews.
- **Insurance Coordination:** If you work with insurance networks or government schemes (CGHS, ESI, etc.), keep their rules handy and train staff on correct billing codes. Ensure no double-billing between cash patients and insurance patients.
- **Periodic Review:** Every year, assess whether your fees are still in line with your costs (especially if input costs rose) and competition. Increase them gradually if needed, with notice.

Insurance and Third-Party Payors

- **Understanding Coverage:** If many patients have insurance or government coverage (insurance like Star Health, or state funds), learn their claim process. Missing claim filings are lost revenue.
- **Network Participation:** Being part of empanelments (e.g., local hospital consortia, telemedicine partners) can increase patient base, but ensure reimbursements are timely.
- **Billing Staff Training:** Errors in insurance claims lead to rejections. Train at least one staff member thoroughly on common insurance protocols and claim submissions.

Investment and Scaling Up

- **Reinvest Profits:** Use part of your earnings to improve your practice. This could be buying a new diagnostic device, adding a piece of office furniture, or training staff. Even a small annual reinvestment (e.g., 5-10% of profits) compounds into significant upgrades over time.
- **Expansion Planning:** If you're considering a second clinic or adding a new specialty, prepare a simple business plan. Estimate costs (rent, salaries) vs expected revenue (based on your current patient flow).
- **Financing Options:** For large investments (e.g., a new ultrasound machine), consider loans from medical banks or low-interest government schemes. Always compare rates and terms.
- **Break-even Analysis:** Before any major spend, calculate how many additional patients or sessions you need to cover the cost. This helps avoid impulsive decisions.

Fundamentals of Practice Management

- **HR and Salaries:** Treat your team well. Set fair wages and timely payments. Happy staff are efficient staff (and turnovers are costly).
- **Inventory Control:** Keep an eye on stock (medicines, disposables). Overstocking ties up cash; understocking can disrupt services. Regularly use inventory lists or simple software.
- **Outsource When Needed:** As revenue grows, you might outsource tasks (like housekeeping, payroll, or accounting). This frees you to focus on strategy and patient care.
- **Legal & Tax:** Ensure timely filing of taxes (GST, IT). Consider hiring a professional accountant or using reliable accounting tools. Staying compliant avoids penalties that can be devastating to small practices.

Your Business Management Toolkit

- **Budget Spreadsheet Template:** A simple Excel sheet with columns for each income/expense category, auto-summing monthly totals. (Could include sample formulas.)
- **ROI Calculator:** For any new equipment, calculate how many extra patients or treatments per month it needs to break even. Use a basic worksheet to input cost, expected usage, and revenue per use.

Key Takeaway

- Treating your practice like a business doesn't diminish your calling – it *sustains* it.
- Ethical financial management ensures you can continue caring for patients tomorrow.
- By tracking your money, budgeting, and smart reinvestment, you build a financially healthy clinic that can grow in scale and quality.

CHAPTER 10

SUSTAINING THE HEALER: WELL-BEING, BALANCE, AND LOOKING AHEAD

> ***"To heal others, we must also remain whole ourselves."***

Medical practice is rewarding, but also demanding. To truly **thrive**, doctors must care for themselves as much as they care for patients. This final chapter focuses on *you*, your well-being, balance, and vision for the future.

Recognizing and Preventing Burnout

Medicine has one of the highest burnout rates. Notice the signs in yourself: chronic fatigue, irritability, or dread of work. You built your career to heal, not to be drained.

Strategies to Avoid Burnout:

- **Work Boundaries:** Set clear working hours. If you promise patients a 6 PM closing, stick to it. Let your team know you won't answer non-urgent calls after a certain time, and enforce it.

- **Delegate:** You don't have to do everything. Delegate paperwork to staff or consider hiring part-time help for evenings. Freeing even an hour each evening for yourself is invaluable.
- **Take Breaks:** It may sound counterintuitive, but short mental breaks during the day improve focus. Step outside for sunlight, have lunch away from your desk, or practice deep breathing between patients.
- **Mental Health:** If stress feels overwhelming, seek support. Talk to colleagues, a mentor, or a counselor. Peer groups or physician support networks can be eye-openers; you'll learn you're not alone in feeling pressure.
- **Hobbies and Social Life:** Maintain interests outside medicine—a sport, art, and time with family. These recharge you emotionally. Many doctors find purpose renewal by volunteering in a non-medical context (e.g., coaching a child's sports team).

Work-Life Integration and Boundaries

Finding harmony between career and personal life is key:

- **Schedule Personal Time:** Treat family or exercise like appointments. Block them in your calendar and honor them.
- **Learn to Say No:** It's okay to decline a conference or committee if it overloads you. Focus on what aligns with your goals and values.
- **Mindful Transitions:** End each day by mentally "wrapping up" work. You might write a quick to-do list for tomorrow and leave it at the office. This symbolic act helps your mind detach.

Mindfulness and Stress Reduction

Small daily practices reduce stress:

- **Mindful Moments:** Spend 5 minutes at your desk doing nothing but breathing deeply before starting clinics. It centers you.
- **Gratitude:** Each day, recall one patient or moment that made you feel good ("Mrs. Kapoor thanked me for explaining her meds again – that felt nice."). This reinforces job satisfaction.
- **Physical Health:** Exercise regularly, eat healthily, and sleep well. A doctor who ignores their own health models bad habits for patients. Even short walks or yoga can boost your mood and energy.

Mentorship and Succession

Consider the future:

- **Find a Mentor:** Even as an experienced doctor, a mentor (senior colleague or a coach) can offer perspective on career choices and challenges. If you're a junior, seek guidance from seniors.
- **Be a Mentor:** Teaching or supervising medical students or younger doctors can be rejuvenating and a form of giving back.
- **Succession Planning:** If you dream of retiring or reducing hours someday, start planning early. Train a junior doctor or assistant who shares your values to take on duties. A staggered handover (e.g., half-days by the successor while you're still full-time) smoothens the transition.
- **Estate and Exit Strategy:** Ensure your practice's continuity. Will someone inherit or buy it? Legal documents and clear plans prevent turmoil when you step back.

The Future of Indian Healthcare

Finally, look outward. India's healthcare landscape is evolving:

- **Digital Health Expansion:** Government initiatives (eSanjeevani, Ayushman Bharat) are expanding telehealth and insurance coverage. Familiarize yourself with leveraging these.
- **Patient Expectations:** As urbanisation grows, patients will expect more convenience and transparency (online bookings, EMRs). You'll likely see younger patients driving changes, so stay adaptable.
- **Community Health:** The next decade will need doctors not just in clinics but also in community health roles (public health, policy, rural outreach). Opportunities exist if you innovate.
- **Lifelong Impact:** Remember the original calling that brought you here – to help and heal. The system will change around us, but the core values of compassion, ethics, and curiosity remain timeless.

Action Points

- Block one personal activity (hobby, family time) into your weekly schedule as non-negotiable.
- Identify one stressor to reduce (maybe try hiring a part-time scribe or automating billing, as earlier chapters suggested).
- Commit to learning something outside medicine monthly (perhaps a relaxation technique like meditation or a digital detox challenge).
- If you have children or juniors interested, share the noble aspects of medicine with them – inspire the next generation as others inspired you.

Final Key Takeaway

- You've come a long way since first donning the white coat.
- You're not alone in feeling the weight of responsibilities.
- **But remember:** The world needs you to thrive, not just survive.
- By balancing systems with empathy, tech with ethics, and work with well-being, you become the true **Medical Marvel,** not just to your patients, but to yourself.
- **The future doctor is a healer and a resilient leader, and that future starts with the small steps you take today.**

Original sources for the studies, surveys, and reports cited

1. **72% of patients want doctors who explain things clearly**: Deloitte, "2020 Global Health Care Consumer Survey" (p. 12): https://www2.deloitte.com/us/en/pages/life-sciences-and-health-care/articles/global-health-care-consumer-survey.html
2. **83% of patients would switch providers after a poor communication experience:** NRC Health, "2021 Consumer Voice of the Patient Report" (chapter on clinician empathy): https://nrchealth.com/resources/consumer-voice-of-the-patient
3. **75% of patients expect a follow-up within a couple of days; two-thirds deem it "irreparable" after a week** – NRC Health, "Top Box Patient Experience Survey" (2022 insights): https://nrchealth.com/resources/top-box-patient-experience-survey
4. **80% of patients choose providers based on easy access** – Accenture, "Digital Health Technology Vision 2021" (figures on consumer convenience): https://www.accenture.com/us-en/insights/health/digital-health-technology-trends

5. **70% of Indian patients say social-media posts influence their health decisions**: Madhup and Kaur, "Influence of social media on health-related decision-making among adults attending an outpatient department of a tertiary care centre in India" (National Medical Journal of India, 2023)
6. **82.9% of Indian adults actively use multiple platforms like WhatsApp and Facebook:** IAMAI & Kantar, "Indian Media and Entertainment Industry Report 2024" (digital usage stats)
7. **94% of patients read online reviews when evaluating doctors**: Digital Authority Partners, "42 Statistics Healthcare Marketers Need to Know in 2024"
8. **84–94% of patients consult review sites to vet providers**: Software Advice, "45 Patient Review Statistics for Healthcare Professionals" (2023)
9. **77% of patients start healthcare searches on Google**: BrightLocal, "2023 Local Consumer Review Survey" (healthcare vertical data)
10. **Practo facilitated 200 million online appointments over 15 years**: Practo, "Practopedia: Your Digital Healthcare Companion" (2024 report)
11. **597 million monthly WhatsApp users in India**: Statista, "Number of WhatsApp users in India 2025"
12. **87% of consumers want more video content from brands**: Wyzowl, "State of Video Marketing 2024"
13. **NEET 2024 applicants: 57% female**: National Testing Agency, NEET-UG 2024 Session Report
14. **36% of first-year Indian medical students were inspired by family in healthcare; 64% by "noble" nature of the profession:** Gupta et al., "Motivational factors influencing the career choice of undergraduate

medical students—A cross-sectional study" (Journal of Clinical and Diagnostic Research, 2022)

15. **14.6% of medical students cite financial security as a motivator:** Jain and Singh, "Career choice factors among medical students in India" (Indian Journal of Medical Ethics, 2021)
16. **50.4% of first-year students chose medicine for social respect/prestige:** Sharma et al., "Attitudes of medical students towards their career choice" (International Journal of Community Medicine and Public Health, 2020)
17. **23% of students entered medicine due to parental influence:** Patel and Desai, "Parental expectations and medical career choice" (Medical Journal Armed Forces India, 2019)
18. **47% of physicians cite regulatory requirements as a burnout factor:** athenahealth, "Healthcare Regulations and Physician Burnout" (white paper, 2022)

BLUEPRINT TO GROWTH

You've got almost like a blueprint of how to build a thriving medical practice in your hands. The Medical Marvel is your map to branding, management, leadership, and non-clinical excellence. Now you have two choices:

Consider this as a map and walk alone, or, if you'd like me to walk beside you, guide you, or answer any questions, you can schedule a 1-to-1 meeting with me at

info@themedicalmarvel.com.

- **Get Free "Wow" Doctor Toolkit Visit: www.themedicalmarvel.com**
- Join MMA Doctors Community

(WhatsApp Channel for updates & learning)

- **Subscribe to Growth e-Newsletter:** write us on **info@themedicalmarvel.com** or visit **www.themedicalmarvel.com**
- **Invite me for a Talk / Bulk Orders: info@themedicalmarvel.com**
- **For More Details:** www.themedicalmarvel.com

- **Instagram Page:**

  https://www.instagram.com/medicalmarvel_/

- **Facebook Page:**

  https://www.facebook.com/medicalmarvel

Your practice has the potential to grow beyond limits. Let's make it happen together.